To Illuminate the Way

To Illuminate the Way

Poems by

Wanda S. Praisner

Kelsay Books

Cover art: Photograph by Wanda S. Praisner
Hotel Al Codega, Venice

Author Photograph: JR Photographers, LLC

ISBN: 978-1-947465-54-1

Kelsay Books
Aldrich Press
www.kelsaybooks.com

I dedicate this collection to my teachers, Sr. Anne Ford and Stephen Dunn, for their early encouragement, kindness, and inspiration, and to my eversupportive family, especially my husband Bob.

Acknowledgments

Grateful acknowledgment to the editors of the following publications in which these poems first appeared, some in earlier versions:

Atlanta Review: "What Remains, Auschwitz"
Ekphrasis: "The Funeral of Shelley"
Edison Literary Review: "Hands Too Small," "The Night a Seventh Grader Came Home Late"
Exit 13: "Occurrence at Nakuru," "The Pera Palace Hotel, Istanbul," "Beneath Bunaken," "In a Parking Lot in Scotland," "Hiroshima Peace Park," "Cobalt Coast Resort," "The Ruins of Angkor," "Grossmutter"
Howl of Sorrow, Poetry Inspired by Hurricane Sandy (Long Branch Arts Council): "After Sandy," "Visiting the Jersey Shore, Six Months after Sandy"
Journal of New Jersey Poets: "Hearts & Cemeteries," "What I Remember," "February Beyond My Window," "Becalmed," "December Twelfth, 2015," "His Chain of Hours"
Kelsey Review: "Driving to Chatham," "The Funeral of Shelley," "Early for a Workshop at the Arts Club, I Go Next Door to Edwin Booth's The Players," "To Illuminate the Way," "Elegy for My Son, Nine Years Later," "Angels"
Lips: "The Flowers of May," "What's Cherished," "Your Voice," "But It's Christmas"
Literature Today: "Listening to the Dial Tone"
Musehouse: "Visiting the Jersey Shore, Six Months after Sandy"
Paterson Literary Review: "At the Hotel Bora Bora," "Lotus Land"
Poets for Living Waters: "Gulf War Disaster: 2010"
Sensations Magazine, Losing a Child Supplement: "Dots I'd Connect"
Stillwater Review: "Back Toward Monado"
The Crafty Poet: "After Love"
The Crafty Poet II: "The Funeral of Shelley"

Tiferet: "Cuba, Body and Soul," "Epilogue: Remembering a Son and Venice"

U.S. 1 Worksheets: "Winter," "Picking a Bouquet of Russian Olive," "After Reading a Line from Dante in a Florence Restaurant," "Son Home from College"

Voices From Here (Paulinskill Poetry Project): "In the Eternal City," "Mother's Day, 2015"

Voices from the Porch Anthology (Main Street Rag): "Tom, We Waited"

World Enough Writers Ice Cream Anthology (Concrete Wolf): "Ice Cream with Whipped Cream for Our Fiftieth"

"Son Home from College" previously appeared in *Sometimes When Something Is Singing.*

"What Remains, Auschwitz" was a Winner in the 2016 *Atlanta Review* International Poetry Competition.

"Visiting the Jersey Shore, Six Months after Sandy" placed 2nd in the 2013 *Musehouse* Poem of Hope Competition.

"At the Hotel Bora Bora" was an Editor's Choice in the 2013 Allen Ginsberg Contest.

"Driving to Chatham," "The Funeral of Shelley," "At the Pera Palace Hotel," "Elegy for My Son, Nine Years Later," "Cobalt Coast Resort" and "Angels" were nominated for a Pushcart Prize.

"His Chain of Hours" won the 2017 New Jersey Poets Prize.

I wish to thank the U.S. 1 Poets' Cooperative, the Artist/Teacher Institute, South Mountain Poets, Peter Murphy's Getaways, and The Frost Place for guiding my efforts in becoming a poet.

Gratitude to the New Jersey State Council on the Arts for its 1995-6 Poetry Fellowship; to the Geraldine R. Dodge Foundation for several fellowships to the Provincetown Fine Arts Work Center and the Virginia Center for the Creative Arts.

My thanks to Stanley Kunitz and Maxine Kumin for their help along the way. My appreciation to Nancy Scott, who read and responded to an earlier version of this manuscript.

Contents

III. Bringing Light to Dark

IV. Flickering Light

Prologue

Ice Cream with Whipped Cream for Our Fiftieth Anniversary

What lies behind us and what lies before us
are small compared to what lies within us.
                    —Ralph Waldo Emerson

All eight of us savor *Eis mit Schlagsahne*
in Leonberg's town square, where we've come
to show children and grandchildren
my father's birthplace, # 18 *Marktplatz,* the half-
timbered house dating from 1711, where his father
had his tinsmith's shop on the ground floor,
later dying in wartime.

"Johannes Keppler lived across the way in the 1500s,"
father would say. A plaque confirms it.
Earlier by our hotel we filmed my grandmother's
house, rural once, now city—
a store, EURO BAZAR, at street level.

This an inward journey as I stare
at my son's jaw line, so like his brother's,
a son lost a quarter century ago.
Love, a joy we borrow.
The church bell tolls another hour.

I. To Illuminate the Way

Black & White Movies

Memory is more indelible than ink.
                              —Anita Loos

I watch them again, films from the 1930s & 40s—
the Great Depression, the war years—
when I could see heaven by blocking out hell,
an escape even now—stories brought to life
before me at a time when I learned those I loved
could look at me with Tyrone Power eyes and lie
& I believed, just as I knew angels hovered, Santa came,
& on weekends Daddy would take us in his DeSoto
to the Liberty in Stapleton for the latest movie:
men in suits, suspenders, fedoras—tuxes & top hats,
women in slinky sequined dresses trailing feathers
& furs, all lighting up like the stars they were, bearing
halos of smoke, saying *Swell!*—& at the end,
fewer than a dozen actors listed; so I knew their names,
even sent to Hollywood for black & white glossies
of them, their heavenly bodies reaching 86 Sheridan Ave.—
Greta, Lana, Hedy—Errol, Cary, Gary—my friends
whose faces & voices I knew; I laughed
with Abbott & Costello, sang with Mickey & Judy,
danced with little Shirley & Bojangles,
Fred & Ginger—Ginger, my idol, whose smile
& hairdo I tried to copy, but it didn't work; & nights
as they dazzled in the sky, ever-present & true,
like family, I remembered them in my prayers
before closing my eyes & dreaming of them.

Night Watchman

The call of the cardinal, dull drone
of a plane, and I'm a child again,
eyes closed, daydreaming,
propped against the clothesline platform
at Grandpa's, where Momma's dropped me off.

Aunt Helen, who lives with Grandpa,
has already reeled out and in his work shirts
and trousers, her full slips and step-ins.
He's out back tending his grape arbor and bee hives.
She's inside marcelling her hair, curling her eyelashes,
stroking makeup on her legs to look like stockings.

I'm safe on my raft in an ocean freed
of pirates and sharks, even U-boats and Nazis,
like Aunt Helen, I too support the war effort.

And land is near. I hear bird calls. Teacher says
the male stakes a territory, knows by instinct
an area can support only one nest.
I can still hear Momma and Daddy's last fight,
he saying Aunt Helen wasn't Grandpa's.
"That worthless uncle of yours, your no-good mother."

But then I remember Aunt Helen's sweet talk
to the parakeet and her latest lost kitten—the nice
servicemen who come as soon as Grandpa leaves
for his job as night watchman at DeJonge's
paper factory over on Brighton Avenue.

The Night a Seventh Grader Came Home Late

When she mounted the stairs
to the second floor apartment,
they were waiting for her—
father in the wing chair,
mother & brother on the couch.

Father bolted toward her,
Where have you been?
Why are you late? Her fright
& silence taken as signs of some kind
of guilt. Didn't they trust her? Know her?

Mother & brother glared,
said nothing as he ranted on and on
about the worry she'd caused.
Then, as a cat tires of pawing a finch,
he finished with her, sent everyone to bed.

These sudden strangers—
lost to her decades later
by death, dementia, & estrangement—
never learned that all the students
at P.S. 29 Recreation went to P.S. 30

to see a film on westward expansion,
recommended by their teacher,
& she didn't call home because
she didn't have a nickel,
& none of the other girls had to.

Remembering

I'd forgotten the 1940s. An old movie shows
USO dances in hangars, local girls unloaded
from backs of supply trucks
into the arms of hooting & whistling GIs
ready to fox trot, jitterbug, follow a conga line
before shipping out.
               We made do & did without—
like the eighth grade graduation parties my friends
planned, I pleading for one: our apartment house
basement would be fine, I'd clean & decorate,
only the cost of chips & cola—no juke box—
I'd borrow records:
          Dick Haymes' & Helen Forest's "Together"
& "Long Ago and Far Away," even Glenn Miller's
"In the Mood." Finally Dad's OK—
details in place like a strategic battle plan—
& I danced with Magne Paulsen & Richie Sorensen
& they kissed me in Spin the Bottle & Post Office.
               Less, more in those days,
days when we saved fat, metal, rubber, always
a salvage drive on, food stamps, gas rationing—
two & a half gallons a week, we went nowhere—
These times are like a bad toothache or childbirth,
Mom said. *You'll forget—*
       & so we did what we could for the boys:
Mom volunteered as a nurse's aide,
Dad painted black eyelids on his Essex's headlights,
I bought war stamps. Uncle Edward, in the army,
& Uncle Willie, the navy, made it back, but never
spoke of it, choosing not to remember.

Thoughts of College Courses

Many of us aced Philosophy 10
without one moment's contemplation—
Plato, Descartes, Kant, et al.,
their conclusions on the human scene.
We tasted, spit back, never digested
their captions on pictures already painted.
Who had appetite for Kierkegaard
and Meister Eckhardt's inner search?
We lunched on English 7's lighter fare:
McCullers' Life is a matter of intake,
elimination, and reproduction
and Joyce's Love is the soul of life.
Life it was we devoured.

I should read them all again, but won't.
that tree falling with no one to hear it.
When it falls you hear it, see it, feel it,
carry it with you a lifetime—
how long it takes a trunk to turn to soil.
I could fill blue books now
on how much better it is to grope
in darkness.
Let in the light, you see the dust.

Aunt Helen

Like a Central Park horse,
Aunt Helen never moved
until it was absolutely
necessary.

But while the horse earned
its slowness and keep,
Aunt Helen simply took hers
at an early age,
adding laziness
like the straw hat
atop the horse's head.

I remember her living
with Grandpa,
pulling her weight
on a route as routine
as her miles per hour.
He did what needed doing.

It was her cats and caged birds
that were closest to her.
She talked and moved
to them
the most.

We were all surprised
when she married
after Grandpa died—
wondering how she managed
so much horsepower.

Lotus Land

But Hollywood today is not the place it was 50 years ago.
—The New York Times, 2/15/15

Because Hollywood made the movies
that highlighted my childhood,
I went west in '59 to teach in Santa Monica,
earning seven thousand, more than twice
my salary in New York City.

Magic *was* there: adorable Debbie Reynolds
shopped alongside me in Bullocks Wilshire;
wholesome Dorothy Maguire said Hi
in the Westwood Hamburger Hamlet restroom,
admired the dress I wore;

glamorous Zsa Zsa Gabor in a neighboring
booth in the Beverly Hilton's romantic
Star on the Roof—she, too, sipped
a seven dollar Dream of Love cocktail,
a peach floating on top.

I floated on high taking a photo of Janet Leigh
at the hotel's reception for *Porgy and Bess*
and when Frank Sinatra drove up grinning
as he kept opening and closing the door,
I knew I'd died and gone to lotus heaven.

Easter lilies and poinsettias grew wild
outside my classroom, though it never rained
and smog hung like homesickness along the shore.

In the Eternal City

for Isabel

In the Galleria Borghese, Pluto's fingers
still dimple Persephone's marble flesh—
her tears haven't moved;

Daphne's still changing into a laurel tree—
large toes rooted, bark covering part
of her body. Ovid wrote Apollo's hand
could still feel her beating heart.

Spring again, dear friend. Still cool.
Newly-potted cyclamen in the Gardens,
fruit trees come out in pinks and white.

We ate tortellini and tartufo.
I bought a statue of a naked child writing in a book;
you tweaked its cherub cheeks.
In a crypt we saw bones of four thousand monks.

You wore red crepe opening night
to the Sleeping Beauty ballet. The last day
we tossed coins to ensure our return—
later went back to see Caravaggio's St. Jerome.

The saint still writes in a book—white-beard,
bald head, a scarlet cloak partly covering his body—
the skull on a scythe-shaped cloth
you said was there to remind us of our mortality.

Occurrence at Nakuru

Kenya, 1980

for Tom

Something's blocked the shallow Makalia—
water overflows its banks.
Your head's down in the safari van
absorbed with your still-wet Polaroids
of two million flamingos
you can't wait to show in school.

From the open roof the ranger points out
what looks like a rolled-up oriental rug
but it's a twelve-foot python stretched
across the narrow river, its middle split,
a pregnant Thomson's gazelle inside.

The ranger reconstructs the scene:
"The gazelle, about to give birth,
was crushed by the reptile. The snake
made the mistake of swallowing it
headfirst. The three-inch horns
caused the fatal wounds."

"But how could it swallow a gazelle?"
you ask. The ranger speaks of jaws
joined by elastic ligaments, dislocating
at will. Not satisfied, you keep on,
the ranger patient as this ancient land,
where the line between life and death
is blurred as a zebra's stripes on the horizon.

"The python gorged itself, died, and fell
into the river, and so it was," he answers.

29

I think of the perfect waiting fetus
not delivered, your attention now
on a warthog in the distance, running
for cover, tail up straight as a flag,
almost camouflaged by savanna grasses—
my telephoto focused on an iridescent
starling flitting safely in and out
the three-inch thorns of an acacia tree.

Son Home from College

for Bobby

Your excited talk at breakfast
is of the bird chatter at sunrise,
the lazy wavering melody
moving through the window.
"It's good to be out of the city!"

I tell of the ten or more finches
in charge of stirring the sun,
the elusive thrush in shadowed
wood we seldom see. I take out
the Peterson guide, and you look on

polite as a guest—our connection
delicate as the spider's strand
we part as we walk in the garden—
sticking, tickling our faces—
my bird songs no longer yours.

You cut the grass, even though I say
you'll be mowing down
the violets. We stand together,
yet apart. Your shadow on the lawn
grown larger than my own.

June, Casement Windows Open Wide

Once again the song of the wood thrush
long absent from my garden.
Life diminished when he left.

Now my dad's voice wafts in from across
the street and for an instant he's alive again.
I imagine him back in his body, checking

his old house: the new circular drive—
grey interlocking stone—added garages,
rooms, windows, doors. A salesman all his life,

he's probably praising the renovations
to the new owner before crossing to my house
to tell me what he really thinks,

the way he'd stop by unexpectedly
after a falling-out with my mother or brother
or when the stock market dropped.

A breeze circles cedars in its arms, brings
the sound of footfalls to the walk, the porch.
Hi dad! How are you? Come in!

To Illuminate the Way

Venice, late November

Rain, though the forecast said sun,
weather unpredictable as the outcomes
of the turns I take through the narrow *calli*—
even with a map, a maze easy to get lost in.
Shop windows agleam with hand blown glass,
decorated masks for *Carnevale.*
We all wear masks to protect our fragile selves.

A warn sun appears as I near the Doges Palace,
though each day, temperatures drop.
Tintoretto's *Paradiso* detains me.
"The world's largest painting." the guide declares.

We're led to the Bridge of Sighs, it grows
dimmer, more and more left behind. Last glimpses
of sky and water through the small metal
latticed windows. Cellblocks. Locked doors.
In one, *1539* etched by an inmate in the marble
below the bars. Such faint light
to accompany the prisoner's dark.

Centuries ago rich merchants brought a servant
to illuminate the way, lanterns fueled
by candles or dried pork rind. I'd like to believe
such a *codega* walks ahead of me—

for even in daylight, the need to move with care
up and down endless bridges: steps chipped,
set at angles, often slippery, and sometimes
a tourist bumps into you to snap that photo
of a boatman poling passengers off and away.
I'd follow that light. I wouldn't stumble.
I'd make it out of the darkness.

II. Plunged into Darkness

Elegy for My Son, Nine Years Later

for Stephen

I keep my eyes from the date
on the board: September 15th—
look instead to the students,
my lesson plans. After the class sings
the national anthem, I remind them
it's the anniversary
of Francis Scott Key penning his poem.
I join in What's New—tell
of white cabbage butterflies I'd seen
among fuchsia gomprenna blooms;
a silver-spotted skipper
sampling sweetness with its feet,

uncoiling, thrusting proboscis in
to draw the liquid out;
and yellow jackets, stirred by the drought,
circling in search of moisture,
like the flies at Aswan Airport
I once swatted, some six hundred
with a folded paper bag.
I say I'll bring in the straw switch
I used in the desert
to keep them from my perspired face.

After class, at the cemetery,
I place roses in a vase, add water.
Yellow jackets near and I remember
I'd forgotten to mention
how the silver-spotted skipper flew,
it's right wing in tatters,
more than half of it gone.

His Chain of Hours

*When a man is asleep, he has in a circle around him the chain
of the hours, the sequence of the years…*
—Marcel Proust

The smell of oranges stacked by the counter
starts the remembrance.
Bizarre images wave in and out
as he waits in line to pay.

Obsessed with circles, he sees them
everywhere. The tawny bubbles
on his cappuccino, tops on the creamers.
They're with him even in sleep.

Knobs, buttons, rings roll in and out,
opening to ovals—what he'd seen or heard
by day linked at random, an encore
before curtained eyes—by morning
the dream sucked away as in an undertow,
pieces left like seaweed or shells.

Last night: the kitchen clock,
with its round face, fallen to the floor
the night he lost his teen-aged son,
restored to its place, ticking, ticking;

a microscope seeing inside the womb
that harbored his son—
the mother still bearing the weight
as though it were a calcified "stone baby."

He is squeezing halves to make juice

38

for his son—how many years ago now?
He has trouble focusing,
seeing them together again
at the oval table—in his hand an orange—
A world as yet intact, he says aloud.

Back Toward Manado

An awful tempest mashed the air...
And black, as of a spectre's cloak
Hid heaven and earth from view
                    —Emily Dickinson

for Bob

Surfacing, I raise my mask,
see you on the dive boat
waving wildly, pointing
back toward Manado—
    the mainland hidden,
    a black & blue cloud cover
    moving our way.

I swim & swim, making little
headway against the current,
and it washes over me again—
    that day you came to my class,
    your face gray as these waters.
    I knew at once
    someone had died.

I stroke & stroke through
the furrowed sea, away from
the safety of reef & shallow water.
    You nodded when I asked
    was it one of our sons,
    & when I asked which one
    you whispered his name.

Sulawesi, Indonesia

40

Beneath Bunaken

Sulawesi, Indonesia

He falls backward into the Celebes Sea.
On other dives his partner was his son,
his new buddy's a stranger.
Life in these waters is different.

He films a pair of Moorish idols,
a deadly blue-ringed octopus.
A large starfish grasps stony coral,
ghost pipefish swim by.

Below the reef wall he moves
from a venomous sea snake,
his mind on the starfish—
the way it regenerates a lost arm.

In a world where one cannot speak,
a speckled moray ribbons out, mouth open.
Surfacing, he strokes toward the boat,
his buddy already on board.

A current cuts through the equatorial water,
chill as the silence at breakfast
when he blurted out the story
of how his son drowned.

Coda

Stephen atop a limestone
outcropping on Great Guana Cay
the summer before he went back
to college. He wears Jams flowered
swim trunks, a school beach towel
capes his bare shoulders.

Sunglasses hang like a necklace,
a water-resistant watch
circles his wrist—behind him a blue sky
catacombed with clouds.

He's not smiling. His lovely mouth
a turned-down arc as he stares
at his father, who's no doubt telling
him where and how to stand.

The picture looks professional.
Someone later asked was he a model
or movie star. It's one of the last
taken before he returned to college,

only to drown in the campus pool.
How tan his body, blond his hair.
The whole of life a letting go—
the past an anchor.

The photo must have been sent off
somewhere when his death was being
written about, because on the back
I wrote his name, and below,
Please return to: my name,
followed by my address.

Dots I'd Connect

Stephen, you now dead
for as long as you were alive—
gone away at nineteen, never to return.
So much can be erased:
Fred Basset from the comics,
the cappuccino at QuickChek,
small dots I'd connect
to get me through the day.
Fred Basset made me smile,
cappuccino was warmth in the hand,
sweetness in the throat
when swallowing was difficult.

The Flowers of May

The way things broken off . . . too soon can last forever.
      —James Richardson

Pansies, petunias, clematis
climbing the holly bush, fragile
violet iris—all purple.

I want to say, Stop!
Stop reminding me
it was my son's favorite color—

a teenager in purple socks,
a purple scarf trailing from his neck.
He never made it to twenty.
His drowning a fishhook in my gut.

Always the waiting, the arrivals—
today he'd be forty-three—
with departures we live.

Mornings and evenings
the sweet lament of wood thrush
recently arrived. Soon
white honeysuckle, white roses.

Everything in Order

There were days I felt almost organized,
like now, en route to share poetry
with sixth graders in New Providence,
I feel good: e-mails answered,
house clean, the holidays still weeks away,

no matter dust already settles or that snow
speckles a gray curbside fist of fur:
a lost squirrel, perhaps a glove—
or that somewhere tracks appear on flagstone,

a door about to be knocked on,
the staccato start of Beethoven's Fifth,
Fate knocking, he wrote,
bringing news no one wants to hear,

or like now, a roadside sign:
GRAVE BLANKETS   WREATHS
to remind me it's time once again
to hang a welcoming circle of greens on the door,
cover my child with bundled balsam, fir and pine.

Driving to Chatham

May 6, 2011

It's easy to smile, sky a blue silk,
dogwoods startling, white.

The VNA sale at the Far Hills Fairgrounds
slows me down, officers directing cars

to fields for parking. Bikers and runners
along 202 bring you back.

And I'm in that pit, that abyss again, Stephen—
you who biked twenty-five miles

to Princeton and back, ran cross-country
in high school, drowned

in your college pool a quarter century ago
training for a triathlon.

Lilac wisteria trails from trees. I miss
my turn, must double back, the way I'll need

to leave this route to hug your brothers
on Mother's Day, loving them even harder,

their wish for me to be happy, knowing
the past was only a moment ago.

Night Run on the Ides of March

for S.J.P. 1967-1986

A spell of warm weather
roused peepers in the pond,
but now a chill breeze stirs
new wind chimes
where the Pernas used to live.

Around the bend, a heady
smell of hearth fire
where the Hammonds were—
evenings still cold.

An opalescent disc disconcerts,
dominates the eastern sky.
From the Big Dipper to Orion's
three horizontal stars,

a mountain of cloud looms.
Once my three young sons
called the belted trio theirs.

Uphill now I slow down, watch
as a towering cloud
overcomes one of them.

Two remain. Once, in Rome
on the Ides of March,
I saw a woman place anemones
at the feet of Caesar's statue.

Now, like a misplaced Milky Way,
a spread of snowdrops

along O'Connor's drive
the Schoenbruns planted.

In the western sky,
I make out the lost star,
a faint blinking
beyond the shroud-like cover.

But It's Christmas

No one needs another
grief poem about a son
drowned in his college pool.

Old news. Except to me.
And I dare not mention him
these decades later

to his father, whose sighs
go deep enough to alarm.
What to do.

But it's Christmas. A purple
bow on our boy's picture,
the house ablaze

in holiday lights, and now,
a live tree—the nursery
man saying to add water

each day, the tree still
alive, even though
it's been cut down.

After a Snowfall

Outside in angled sun,
two bluebirds flit in and out vines.
Resident deer rest below,
face the back of my neighbor's house—

he's moved to a retirement home,
not here to see them—the house
empty, still unsold. It's said
a house dies when no one lives in it.

Snow igloos my garden gnome,
the red ribbon around its neck,
much as snow mounds Stephen's grave,
a silver cross around his.

Sun, now past its zenith, and I,
weary from shoveling,
begin to lower for a nap.
Heat ticks in baseboards,

my body eases, leaves me, slips away
like ice in sun. I am butter melting
on the pancakes he loved
as I let go into the light.

Tom, We Waited

Green Turtle Cay, the Bahamas, July 2012

Tide changed high to low, sand bars exposed.
I took your children to the beach along a path
ripe with sea grapes, coral ixora, white oleander
as we waited word of your boat injury—
your father planted by the phone, pen and paper near,
immobilized as you were, strapped to a board,
gasping in pain, the island nurse injecting you.

Men gave you oxygen, carried you down
flights of stairs, you and your frightened wife
loaded onto a truck, a ferry to a doctor, x-rays.
I looked out to sand like silk, an Abaco parrot
upside-down in a gumbo-limbo tree,
skeletal rattling of wind in palms.

Then news you were on a chartered plane
to a Nassau hospital: four shattered ribs,
a punctured lung—air in your chest cavity.
We waited till you returned to us.
A curly-tailed lizard still looked for bugs
on our porch as we ate, I still saw
the newspaper photo of your brother being wheeled
on a gurney from the pool, the ground opening,
we plunged into darkness, earth closing over us.

Mother's Day, 2015

One son's in Connecticut,
one's visiting a friend
in Germany,
one died.

Because I'm grateful
for what remains,
I spend the day watching
old movies.

A.M.: *Stella Dallas*—
Barbara Stanwyck.
I'm filled up
at film's end. Next,

Imitation of Life—
Lana Turner
and her jewels—
her best friend, "Steve."

P.M.: *The Talented
Mr. Ripley;* if only
Matt Damon didn't
look like my Steve.

Epilogue: Remembering a Son and Venice

Just weeks ago in Venice my grandchildren
lit candles for him in an ancient church;
I took a photo of a last perfect coral rose
in a sheltered courtyard. Years ago in this city
he bought a gold Cartier band; he ran
with his brother through the narrow streets at night.

Once it hurt too much to remember, being
bereft of him. Eyes, greener than the sea, a sea here
in New Jersey I visit with his brother on December days
when rhododendron leaves curl into themselves
and hang like prisms from a chandelier.
I place lighted candles in windows,
wrap gifts for the nephews and niece he never knew.

III. Bringing Light to Dark

Listening to the Dial Tone

for Isabel and Lu

When I heard you were in the hospital,
I searched out old photos of you—
holding our Stephen at his christening,
the two of us in Monte Carlo's
Café Rouge—with our husbands
canoeing down the cold Delaware.

We hadn't seen one another in years—
warm exchanges on Christmas cards
our sole connection
though we lived only a town apart.
Too late now to say it was you
I called when Stephen died.

Nothing left but to phone your husband,
speak of your surgery, coma—
pretend not to notice when his voice
falters and he has to hang up.
Nothing left but to listen to the dial tone
after we're disconnected.

The Pera Palace Hotel, Istanbul

And I say it is as good
to be a woman as to be a man
                    —Walt Whitman

for Dikmen

My Turkish friend pours Kakut Kavaklidera
as we dine along the Bosporus on squid,
Bay of Marmara bass, baklava and pears—
insists we visit the Pera Palace Hotel,
"Our city's first elevator!"

From Sirkeci Station we climb Galata Hill
to the hotel where I film the coral marble
lobby, the palanquin used a century ago
to transport Europe's aristocracy
after they stepped off the Orient Express.

"Jackie O was a guest," she says,
as we move through corridors, noting
brass door plaques: 103 Greta Garbo,
104 Mata Hari, 114 Empress Elizabeth
of Austria, 411 Agatha Christie.

Above the reception area she points out
narrow balcony windows
used by harem women, allowed to watch.
Then Atatürk's suite, 101: his portrait, bed,
an embroidery predicting his time of death.

My friend, who supports his vision
for a more modern Turkey, counsels women
on their rights, teaches them English,
reads them Whitman, tells me that daily
her life is threatened by fundamentalists.

In a Parking Lot in Scotland

A man waits for his wife to return
from the Ayrshire Business Center,
begins to nod off.

A woman pulls alongside, locks up,
crosses to the Hospice shop,
arms full of donations.

The West Highland terrier she's left
inside the car, now jumps onto the back
window ledge to better view its mistress,

who soon disappears.
It stares at the vacated space,
giving itself wholly to this attention,

and nothing else matters—
neither a train whistle, nor cars
coming and going. A spring coiled, ready,

waiting—a firecracker soon to explode
in rapture at the moment of her return.
In the other car, the man has fallen asleep.

What I Remember

November 8. 2003

We live in our lives, day by day,
someone said, but I mark mine by nights.

A lifetime of running out there alone, free,
earth and sky mine for the length of the run—
no two ever the same—weather, the seasons.

And this week, two firsts: an aurora borealis—
white flares spearing northward
into a pink sky; tonight, a lunar eclipse.

Later, from the college Union's wall of glass
I looked out to anchored ships in the Narrows,

the Manhattan skyline on the left,
the Verrazano's green lights on the right.

Running now under a moon returned,
what I remember is the sparrow on its side
on the ledge outside the windows,

impaled by the thin four-inch-high rods,
meant to keep it away—

wind ruffling its feathers, so for a moment
it seemed it was still moving.

At the Hotel Bora Bora

Outriggers brought in the performers
for last night's show.

Hips swiveled, circled in yucca leaves—
mother-of-pearl arcs around bronze necks,
breasts cupped in coconut shells.

A week now since I felt
the lump under my arm.

Men in loincloths, bare tattooed buttocks
twirled circles of flame—

knees moved in and out to the drums,
bodies wet, sweat dotting the sand.

My love sunbathes on the deck
of our above-water bungalow.

I picture home: trained hands,
palpation, an ultrasound.

Blades of the ceiling fan blur together
like days that come, then are gone—
what was, never to return.

Through the window in the floor,
gray mullet gather like storm clouds.

Hands Too Small

"Nimble fingers make sneakers,
carpets and bricks," a guide says.
"They cut and dye
chicken feathers for shuttlecocks,

they sharpen surgical instruments.
Three-to-six-year-olds work needles
longer than their fingers,
their hands too small for scissors."

All day, twelve-year-old Mahotra
stitches together hexagonal
leather pieces for soccer balls.
He earns sixty cents.

Peshgi sits on concrete in a dark
dust-filled room, breathes metal particles.
Malnourished, his teeth rot,
red tinges his hair. He smiles at us.

Tariq hacks up sputum
as he squats before a loom.
He strives to do good work
so the master will not beat him.

Some are branded, even blinded
as punishment for trying to go home.
They do not know their parents
have already sold them.

The Ruins of Angkor

Siem Reap, Cambodia, 2005

The smell of lemongrass
as the tour begins. Wren-like
prinia flit in & out betel palms
& cashew trees. I film it all.

Angkor Wat's beehive towers, amber
in morning light; sandstone blocks
with holes for roping, lugged by
45,000 elephants from Kulen Hills,
forty-five miles away.

Thousands of Apsara carvings
in this wat alone. "Their earthly
counterparts beguile nightly
in local shows," says Sothy, my guide.

Banteay Srey, Bayon, Angkor Thom.
Ta Prohm's jungle complex
where massive banyan, silk-cotton
& strangler fig trees grow from towers—
roots grotesque, like hardened lava.

I sweet-talk an elephant on a path,
& it turns to look at me.
Driving back, bicyclists in face masks
on both sides of the raised dirt road
under construction--

women in kerchiefs & straw hats
hand-place stones, others work
knee-deep in flooded rice paddies.
Stupas hold bones from killing fields.

Sothy says an American woman
was killed here in '94,
along with her guide & driver,
& six policemen sent to protect her.
The Khmer Rouge wanted her camera

After Reading a Line from Dante in a Florence Restaurant

Love which moves the sun and the other stars.
                    —Dante Alighieri, *Paradiso*

for N. L.

Dante's not the only one
to have lost a first love.
Gentle memories stir

as I savor tortellini en brodo
below a mural of him
watching his smiling Beatrice
walk by for the last time.
My love, raven-haired,
a lodestar—

a measure of me lost
when he left—
no tomorrow, ours.

A lifetime come and gone
like a plane's fading
trajectory, stars navigating
a charcoal sky,
the tracery of heavenly bodies
that rise and fall each day.

It is said we steer star to star,
not land to land.
What solace in paradise?

I have learned life is stones
as well as flowers—
I not there to murmur
him gone.
No, Dante's not
the only one.

Homecoming, 2007

Live to the present through which all future
plunges to the past.
                              —James Joyce

for N.L.

You'd have liked being here today,
rain ended, sun blinking through,

wind flopping the tent, sweeping
away plastic cups, anything
not tied down.

But you've left us.
A leap from your apartment roof.

We said Hello here last year,
the first time in half a century—

you the star quarterback
whose gold Delta Nu pin
I wore over my heart.

Today, the tomorrow
we couldn't see yesterday.

You once said
you could stand any pain
as long as it didn't last.

Early for a Workshop at the Arts Club, I Go Next Door to Edwin Booth's the Players

Leftovers from Booth's life: a round stone brooch,
daggers, a crown from *Julius Caesar.* Thoreau said
wherever men have lived there's a story to be told.

A bust of him as *Hamlet* graces the front room
facing Gramercy Park. As a teenager he toured
with his father, cared for props, costumes—

kept him sober—learned the lines, his own delivery
more sensitive, subdued.

Sargent captured Booth's magnetism, intense eyes
in the life-sized portrait above the mantle.

Steep flights to the third floor, mahogany banisters
carved newels, paintings of actors angled up the stairs.

The single amber-canopied four-poster brass bed
in which he died, slippers alongside.

The bed, where for years sleep eluded him,
where he smoked a pipe during the "vulture hours,"
midnight to dawn, haunted by his brother's epic crime.

At the workshop the poet tells us to think of a house,
its rooms, artifacts. Write about who lived there.

Gulf Oil Disaster: 2010

Before you relax on your beach towel,
erase from memory the image
of that oil-coated pelican in Louisiana
trying to take flight. Never mind its wild eyes,
its weight cemented to East Grand Terre Island.

Wear dark glasses. Lie back. Allow sand
to bear the imprint of your body, a body
covered in sun lotion. In the rhythm
of sea meeting shore, inhale deeply.

In the way a wave removes footprints
from sand, rid your mind of what you read:
More than 500 dead birds found.
Smell salt air, feel spindrift on your face—
subdue unrest. Try to forget. Dare to sleep.

Winter

A foot of snow upholsters
the garden bench. Yard-long
icicles, thick as cudgels
fringe the living room window,
drip to different beats. Inside,

a bouquet of spring flowers
burdens the air—another
family funeral: lilies
already bruised, roses
droop, iris shrivel to crepe,

no matter I cradled the vase
in my arms on the way home.
Death that comes from nowhere
yet reigns everywhere.
The departed who sat here

I lose all over again.
They take hold, adhere,
the way ice cubes in a freezer
cling to fingers. They file past
in cadence and I begin to count.

Hearts & Cemeteries

On that trip through England,
my sons refused to turn south
to go see Shelley's heart in Bournemouth,
so we kept on westward
to the Tank Museum and the Dorset
country road where Lawrence of Arabia
crashed his motorcycle. After
their return home, I paid homage
to Shelley's heart, even visited
Keats House in Hampstead.

Now in the Protestant Cemetery in Rome,
I pay respects to their bones and ashes—
one heart here, the other in England—
a copy of Keat's poetry found
in Shelley's pocket after he'd drowned.
They, young as my sons once were,
left home and never returned—that time
of discovery, becoming—anything possible—
when it's impossible to believe Death
could be a companion on the journey.

The Funeral of Shelley

Louis Edouard Fournier. *Oil on canvas, 1889*

I prefer the painting's fictive depiction
to the gruesome reality.
Something about the poet's early tragic
death being what was really important.
Shelley, life-like, as though asleep
on the crematory pyre at shoreline,
Mary kneeling in the background.
But it wasn't so.
                        When washed up
that summer day, his bloated body
was unrecognizable—no face, no hands.
Italian law mandated a blanketing of lime,
immediate burial in the sand. Weeks later,
it took an hour and a long trench to locate,
excavate him on the day of his cremation—
a metal furnace lugged out to the beach.
                        Leigh Hunt, grief-stricken,
remained in the coach; poor Byron
soon wandered off and swam to his boat,
the *Bolivar,* getting badly sunburned—
his Shelley gone, "the *best* and least selfish
man I ever knew," he said. Mary Shelley
wasn't there. Trelawney plucked his friend's
carbonized heart from the ashes,
later gave it to her.

I like how the artist made the story his:
the bleak winter scene, muted colors,
gray somber tones of sky, water,
windswept beach; the black waiting carriage;
the mourners—among them Trelawny, Hunt,

and Byron in dramatic grieving poses;
the wretched bundled branches.
Smoke blows toward and beyond
a distant wide and high horizon line.

After Love

for Bob

I don't know where my body ends
and yours begins—whose stomach
rumbles. Two become one—like
the Monterey jack I melted

on crackers for our chilled
Pinot Grigio—not easy to separate—
like fifty years together.
It's silent. No phone or clock. No

outside sounds of jet or truck—
knocks on the door—Parcel Post
or FedEx delivering a package.
You're on your back, holding me.

I'm on my left side, right leg
bent, resting on your thighs,
right hand on your heart.
I doze off to the pulse of the heat

coming on, water rushing through
pipes—glad to lose thoughts
of the day that will come and go,
taking one of us with it.

You stir, as though entering
my mind, but no. I wake to your
weight—the stillness broken only
by the sound of our breathing.

Angels

Newtown, Connecticut, December 14, 2012

Childhood is the kingdom where nobody dies—
—Edna St. Vincent Millay

Friday morning on 84, driving
New Jersey to Connecticut
to babysit our grandchildren for a week,
you point to an exit sign:
"Hey—there's another Sandy Hook!"
and I remember taking our young sons
on outings to the Jersey Shore.

We arrive an hour later to the news on TV:
twenty first grade children,
six adults shot and killed
in Sandy Hook Elementary School.
Our grandchildren move closer.

The monsignor at Saint Rose of Lima Church,
one of the first clergy on the scene,
says six or seven were parishioners.
"One was going to be an angel
in our Christmas pageant next week."

In Saturday's paper: the killer, as a boy,
had attended seventh grade
in Saint Rose of Lima School;
used his mother's registered guns;
she, the first victim, shot repeatedly in the face.
Her mother, in Florida, unable to make
a statement to the press.

Below the high school podium bearing
the presidential seal for his Sunday visit,
twenty-six small, white, lit candles.
Along roadsides, cutout angels
begin to appear.

After Sandy

Mantoloking, February 2013

We rented a house here
the summer after we married—
fifty years ago. On visits,
my dad floated in the canal

on an inflated inner tube,
his dachshund across his lap.
On rainy days my mom
read detective magazines.

Four months since Hurricane
Sandy turned the Jersey Shore
into a war zone. Two-hundred
of five-hundred and fifty

borough houses, gone.
In nearby Normandy Beach,
oceanfront wooden stairs
leading nowhere.

Sandra Witkowski has returned
to her Mantoloking home—
still terrified of another storm—
says she can see the shell

of a neighbor's house
from her front door, and from
the back, a house sitting
in the middle of Barnegat Bay.

When introducing herself
these days—she, who shares
a nickname with the hurricane—
says, "I'm Sandra."

Visiting the Jersey Shore, Six Months after Sandy

late April 2013

A great horned owl nests in my surviving
sycamore. Trees become bouquets,
like every spring, startle in pink, white—

even in Mantoloking, ravaged by Sandy.
A house sits in the bay. Others split, halved,
toppled—the intact, water-damaged,

marked with Xs for demolition.
Broken houses that will never again
hold window boxes of petunia, geranium.

Everywhere bulldozers, front-end loaders,
workers removing sand and debris.
Small satellite Home Depots spring up.

All this renewal Prince Harry will see
on his visit in early May, though by then
the house in the bay will be gone;

he'll tour with Governor Christie,
who proposes wider beaches—
an unbroken high and massive sand dune.

In Lavallette, The Crab's Claw Inn
now reopened, operates almost as usual—
though no salad. "We lost some refrigeration,"

says the hostess. I can't take my eyes off
her armful of forsythia, yellow as the sun
restoring earth in spite of everything.

IV. Flickering Light

What's Cherished

On my fingers, my wedding rings,
and my mother's
I'll wear to a gala. I still keep
them in their gray velvet boxes.

When you can afford diamonds
they're worn on old hands,

my father once said, looking at hers.
She glanced down,
then settled her eyes on her rings.

My husband, on seeing mine, says,
They should be left in the safe deposit box.

I flaunt them alongside blue veins,
brown age spots, and of late, purple bruises
from blood-thinners. I bring them out
to remember that once

passion and pleasure lived—and love.
Yes, love placed them on our fingers.

February Beyond My Window

Under a foot of snow, small spruce
seem grotesque, over-costumed
like characters in a Chinese opera.
Red maples bound in icy ligature,
become glass filigree.

Icicles decorate junipers
where cardinals, masked for a ball,
and myrtle warblers wearing
yellow and black, flit in and out.

I spot a bluebird perched on a vine,
the first to visit in fifty years—though
just because you don't see something,
doesn't mean it isn't there.
All magicians know this.

I like the way it stays awhile, nibbling
in the holly or hopping on frozen snow
before flying off, only to return, as I do
again and again to my writing
to see what may have been overlooked—

only now I'm even more distracted,
sensing I'm part of this scene—winter,
death itself, yet hand in hand with life.
I am part of this lasting marriage—

these birds finding sustenance
in a crystal landscape, striving
to stay alive till spring. I am part of all this.
I am part of this all because
I am.

Cobalt Coast Resort

Grand Cayman Island, 2014

Poolside piña colada, the sound
of waves reaching land, scuba tanks
being filled, plunked down.

Bright green iguanas
scamper over black rocks
edging the sandy beach.

Sea grape leaves, flat and upright
against the sky, seem like palms
of hands saying, "Stop!"

I spot a gray patrol boat barring
a small open wooden makeshift craft
from coming ashore—blue, tub-like,

no mast—some forty people aboard,
both moving out of sight
toward Boatswains Bay.

"Cuban migrants," says Arie,
the dive resort owner.
"They come every few weeks now,

but can't stay, or they'll be taken
into custody, repatriated.
Most keep on to Honduras.

I've asked to go visit them,
take games," he says, "but it's not
allowed. No, they can't stay here."

Cuba, Body and Soul

Round dark drops from a sycamore
dot the gravel path, less dusty now
after last night's rain, the sky still bloated
with cumulous clouds in which a jet appears—
an inch or so in size—then is gone.
It reminds me of the bee hummingbird
I filmed in Cuba last week—
an inch or so in size—long bill, wings back.

On the way to see one in the Zapati Wetlands,
our tour bus passed a woman dressed in white—
sun hat to sandals for Santeria—
white worn for a year to purify the soul.

I'd like my soul to be pure, free from sin
and wrongdoing, bride-like when it rises
free of earth's dust and mine into the heavens
toward what may be reachable.
I'd like it to be white and round as the wafer
a priest places on a moist tongue—
the disc dissolving, disappearing
as if it had never been there.

Picking a Bouquet of Russian Olive

Their spicy-sweet fragrance reaches me
before I'm at the empty lot. Two weeks
early. They usually bloom in May.

I snap branches off these invasive trees,
being careful of thorns. Our home
will smell like Polynesia.

Walking back, I notice a pair of ladybugs
mating on one of the centimeter-or-so-
sized leaves. The one on top has ten spots
and is redder than the one underneath—
more orange, mostly hidden.

At our drive, my husband rests
on a garden bench—he's forgotten
to mow the lawn. This morning
he went outside to "go home," pjs, shoes,
a National Geographic underarm.

I said he should shower, breakfast was ready.
"Where's the shower?" he asked,
and I showed him, told him he *was* home.

Last night, despite his twitchings
and bad dreams, he reached for me—
remembered love.

Becalmed

Old age, when we lose ourselves
little by little, was denied you—
after anesthesia, you left in an elsewhere:

you barely talk, have forgotten
time, numbers, how to reason,
how to remember—

gone, our days of exploring the world,
we now becalmed, adrift in a new one,
the billow of our sails stilled,

yet we remain afloat, I now at the helm,
the sea, like time, unfathomable—
the past, an ocean

we can no longer lay anchor in,
though we might glimpse
a young couple, luminous in love,

iridescent fireflies flitting above
the green water, flickering light
as they turn into each other—

where I navigate when it's darkest—
like when they play our song
and you no longer know it—
when I hold onto the stars.

December Twelfth, 2015

To Sinatra, a microphone is as real
as a girl waiting to be kissed.
                                        —E.B. White

Random news items today: a warbling
painted bunting spotted in Prospect Park;
the fear of being buried alive peaked
in the 1740s—cords & bells used;
Ol' Blue Eyes' written notes lacked
capitals because he was too impatient
to press the key—but the soles
of Frankie's shoes were shined.

He'd be 100 today—said early on,
"I was born on the 12th day
of the 12th month," called himself
"a saloon singer" when he worked
in his father's Hoboken bar.

His sweet lyric baritone, the subtle
elegant nuances, how it caressed
the mike. He grew up
crooning with big bands,
could extend his breath,
knew exactly where the beat was.
No one could sing a song better than
Frank Sinatra, said Mel Tormé.

Teenagers in parked cars in the 1940s
came alive to his bell-like tones,
he, cool & natural, in spite of the heat.
In bobby socks & loafers we believed
the man behind the voice was kissing us.

He had much to do: women to love
& marriage (he called his children
every night between five & six);
his search for deeper expression
(an Oscar for dramatic acting).

"When I sing, I believe," he said.
And we did. We do.
He's buried in Palm Springs.
In his casket: Tootsie Rolls, Life Savers,
a bottle of Jack Daniel's. Style, real style.
My kind of guy. His favorite toast:
"May you live to be 100
and may the last voice you hear be mine."

Your Voice

for Gail Fishman Gerwin

You gone? Impossible! We'd chat
before reading at the same venues.
Once, I complimented your melodious
voice, sweet as a fairy godmother's,

while mine croaked like a toad's,
the need to keep clearing my throat.
You handed me a packet of cough drops,
said, "Keep them."

When I noticed you'd lost weight,
I cautioned about getting *too* slim.
I didn't know. How to not look for you
at a next reading, wait to hear your voice.

It's October. Colder. In a jacket pocket
I find your Fisherman's Friend lozenges—
and I see your generous smile, hear
you reading your poems,

a legacy, left us. Your words:
I captured mothers, aunts, sisters
who may have gone to their rest
without my daily rays of hope.

What Remains, Auschwitz

*I was allowed...to work under the greatest son that my people
produced in their 1,000 year history. I regret nothing.*
                                        —Rudolf Hess

In a Warsaw hotel window I saw myself
lick my finger to pick up poppy seeds
and crumbs from the plate,
something Grossmutter did
on her visits from Germany before the war
as we savored her pork roasts and sauerkraut.

Verschwende nichts! I learned well, wasted
nothing—Grossvater's command
to turn off lights when leaving a room,
my father's *Never leave the icebox door open!*

What remained were scraps of fabric
Grossmutter salvaged
from American church friends
and Grossvater's pipe,
as well as the Leonberg newspapers
he'd read and reread in our basement—
the receipts of every bill my father paid.

Now in the State Museum in Oświęcim,
huge display cases: uncountable
pots and sieves, in another,
baby clothes and pacifiers,
then a mountain of black suitcases,
names lettered in white—camp ledgers
listing arrivals, punishments, deaths.

Shoes, high heels, clogs and boots,
prosthetics, prayer shawls, brushes.
Real hair in Room 5,
gray now from Cyclon B,
bolts of coarse lining made from it.
Mounds of dark curls
on closer look are metal spectacles.

The best went to the Vaterland,
SS families, valuables to the Reichsbank,
the rest burned as the Allies neared.
I stand by the remains, regret everything,
my reflection inside the glass case,
rooted in the waste.

Grossmutter

Photos of her Leonberg house I took
on our golden wedding anniversary trip,
bring her back. She, my most distant relative,
closest to me. A story-teller, a star I orbited
on her visits to us—when she discovered Manhattans—

on return flights, even in her eighties
holding up a card printed: MANHATTAN, BITTE
when the stewardess asked, *Kaffee, Tee, oder Milch?*—
later writing she was moved to the last empty row
where she could sing her hymns and yodel.
My fingernails and feet are like hers.

I went to see her when I was twenty, snapped
a last black and white picture of her waving goodbye
from her upstairs window—a fly zigzagging in
to her *Apfel Kuchen*, to rest perhaps on the pillow
she embroidered: *Nur eine Viertelstunde*—
only a quarter hour—her nap time,

when her head dropped to her neckline lace,
the oval garnet brooch she left me:
gold filigree, trumpet clasp.
I called out, *Auf Wiedersehen*,
until we meet again, before turning to leave.

My Father's House

Das Haus ist mein, und doch nicht mein,
nach meir kehrt ein anderer ein...
     —Old German saying

A lifetime of leftovers heap
the dumpster on his drive—
inside, only a wooden broom handle

remains on a hall closet shelf,
despite painters, floor men.

The cup hook my father turned
and turned into one end of it
so he could lower the attic stairs.

All that's left of him in a house
that no longer smells of him.

Once he said he loved
his mother's smell, would savor it
on yearly trips back to Leonberg.

His words echo through empty rooms
in this old house with new smells.

I connect the cup hook to the ceiling
eye hook, where it hangs waiting
for someone else to use it.

The house is mine, and yet isn't
after me another lives in it.

Hiroshima Peace Park

I go to the gift shop to buy a book on Sadako
for Sarah, my twelve-year-old granddaughter—
the age I was when I first saw
the Japanese flag in movie newsreels.

It was said the city would never again be habitable.
Just weeks later, oleander bloomed.
I am not able to look at photographs of destruction,

stop instead at a showcase of colorful origami birds
the size of my fingernail, made by Sadako—
told she had leukemia
nearly a decade after the black rain fell.

She believed if she folded a thousand cranes
the gods would make her well. A year later
a photo of the twelve-year-old in her casket
with her Kokeshi doll, flowers, paper birds.

White doves are released on the anniversary.
"At night," a guide says,
"families light candles in rice paper lanterns
for loved ones lost that summer day."

I picture them launched on the Ohta River,
flowing out to sea,
bringing light to dark like an armada of fireflies.

About the Author

Wanda S. Praisner, a recipient of fellowships from the NJ State Council on the Arts, the Geraldine R. Dodge Foundation, The Provincetown Fine Arts Work Center, and the Virginia Center for the Creative Arts, won the Egan Award, Princemere Prize, Kudzu Contest, First Prize in Poetry at the College of NJ Writers' Conference, and the 2017 New Jersey Poets Prize. A fourteen-time Pushcart Prize nominee, she has been a featured reader at the Governor's Conference on the Arts and at the Dodge Poetry Festival. Her work has appeared in such journals as *Atlanta Review, Lullwater Review,* and *Prairie Schooner.* In 2010 she was inducted into the Curtis High School Hall of Fame, and in 2012 she received an Alumni Fellow Award from Wagner College. A resident of Bedminster, NJ, she is a poet in residence for the NJ State Council on the Arts.

E-mail address: praisner1@verizon.net

Other Books by the Author

A Fine and Bitter Snow (Palanquin Press, USCA, 2003)

On the Bittersweet Avenues of Pomona, Winner, Spire 2005 Poetry
   Chapbook Award (Spire Press, 2006)

Where the Dead Are (CavanKerry Press, 2013)

Sometimes When Something Is Singing (Antrim House, 2014)

Natirar (Kelsay Books, 2017)

www.ingramcontent.com/pod-product-compliance
Lightning Source LLC
Chambersburg PA
CBHW071102090426
42737CB00013B/2442